I Am *an* Artist

by Pat Lowery Collins
illustrated by
Robin Brickman

THE MILLBROOK PRESS
BROOKFIELD, CONNECTICUT

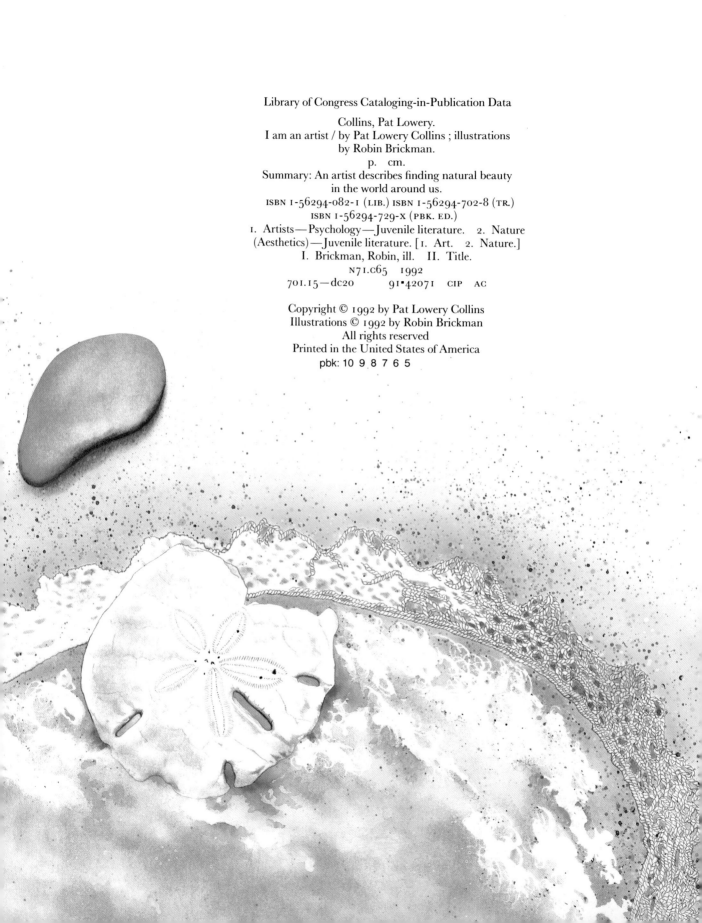

Library of Congress Cataloging-in-Publication Data

Collins, Pat Lowery.
I am an artist / by Pat Lowery Collins ; illustrations
by Robin Brickman.
p. cm.
Summary: An artist describes finding natural beauty
in the world around us.
ISBN 1-56294-082-1 (LIB.) ISBN 1-56294-702-8 (TR.)
ISBN 1-56294-729-X (PBK. ED.)
1. Artists—Psychology—Juvenile literature. 2. Nature
(Aesthetics)—Juvenile literature. [1. Art. 2. Nature.]
I. Brickman, Robin, ill. II. Title.
N71.C65 1992
701.15—dc20   91-42071 CIP AC

For Phoebe
P. L. C.

For Alyce Alpine Neukirk
R.B.

I am an artist when I follow a line where it leads me.

I am an artist when I find a face in a cloud

or watch the light change the shape of a hill.

I am an artist when I discover shadows made
by the moon

or trace patterns in the sand

or when I name the colors inside a shell.

I am an artist when I look through a sun shower
for a rainbow.

I am an artist when I find one.

I am an artist when I notice that the sea is
a mirror for the sky

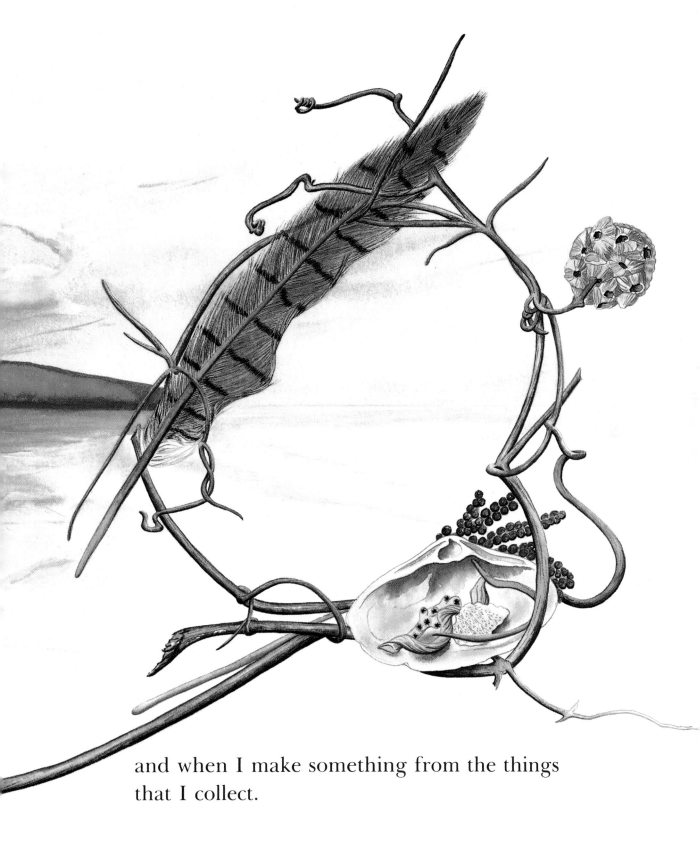

and when I make something from the things
that I collect.

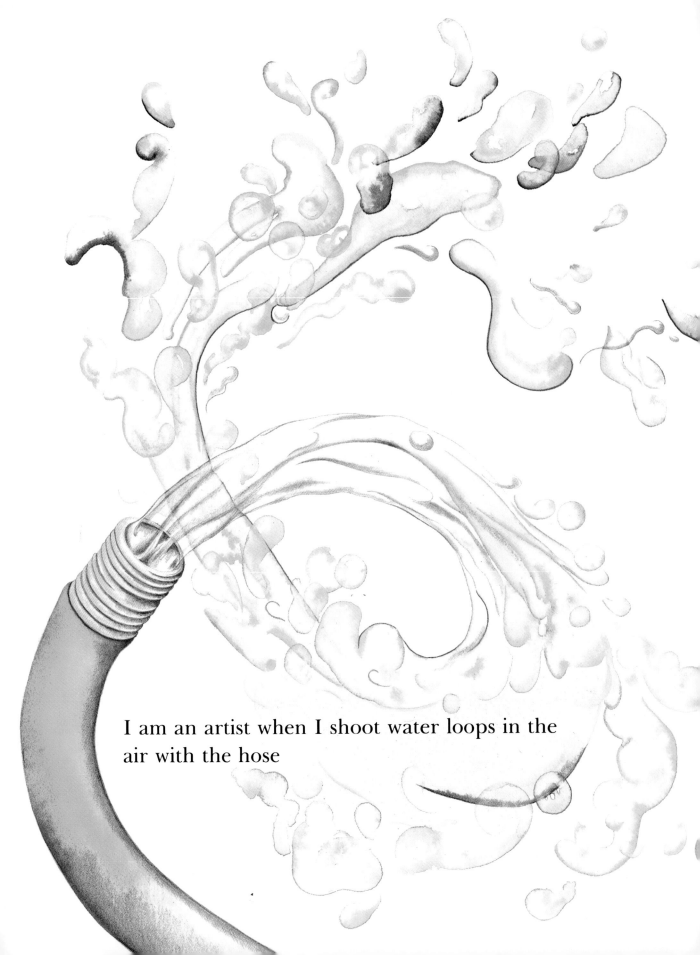

I am an artist when I shoot water loops in the air with the hose or discover pictures in drops of rain.

I am an artist when I cut an apple to see the star inside

or when I watch sunlight turn dust to glitter.

I am an artist when I crunch through crusted snow

and stop to gather winter's hush around me.

I am an artist when I look at a bird until I feel
feathery too

and at an orange until I know what it is to be perfectly round.

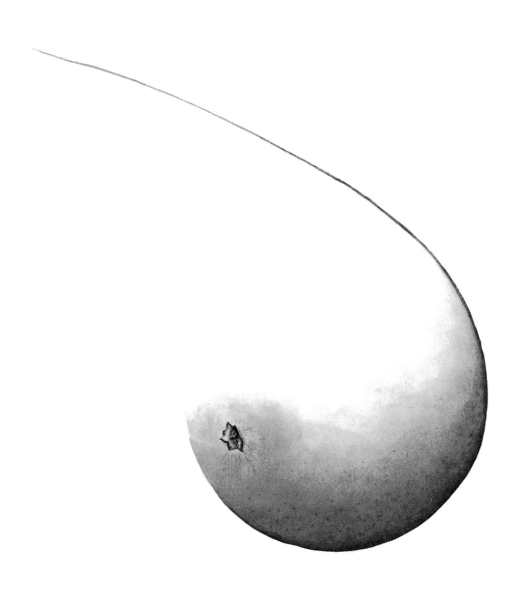

I am an artist when I run my fingers over a
shiny pod or across the rough bark of a tree or

when I blow on a full-blown milkweed and it
splinters into tiny white puffs

or when I pick up a maple-tree seed and send it spinning back to earth by its twin propellers.

I am an artist when I see that the sun comes up
in a soft haze

and goes down in a fiery blaze.

I am an artist when I wait for a star to streak
through the night sky

or when I sit very still in the woods and listen.

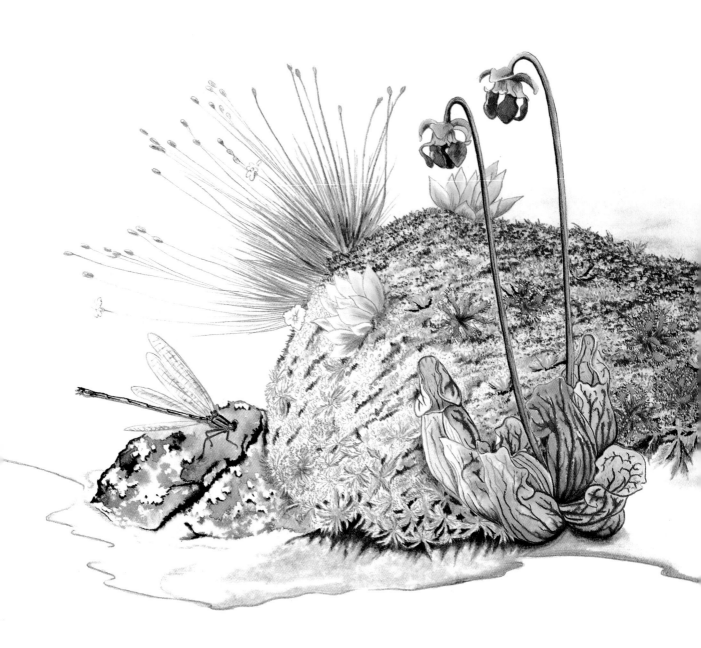

I am an artist whenever I look closely at the
world around me.

And whenever *you* listen and search and see,

you are an artist too.